GREAT WORKS OF
BIBLICAL ART

Douglas Mannering

A Compilation of Works from the
BRIDGEMAN ART LIBRARY

SIENA

Biblical Art

This edition first published in 1995 by
Parragon Book Service Ltd
Units 13-17 Avonbridge Industrial Estate
Atlantic Road
Avonmouth
Bristol BS11 9QD

ISBN 0 75250 841 5

Printed in Italy

Editors: Barbara Horn, Alexa Stace, Alison Stace, Tucker Slingsby Ltd and
Jennifer Warner.
Designers: Robert Mathias and Helen Mathias
Picture Research: Kathy Lockley

The publishers would like to thank Joanna Hartley at the
Bridgeman Art Library for her invaluable help.

BIBLICAL ART

THE BIBLE STANDS right at the heart of the western tradition, in art as in many other aspects of life and thought. This remains true even in our supposedly secular age. Whether or not they realize it, non-believers make use of biblical proverbs and turns of speech, and biblical characters from Adam and Eve onwards still figure in the popular stock of myths.

As the selection in this book indicates, many of the world's great paintings have been dedicated to religious subjects. Most works based on the Bible have been by Christian artists, since other 'peoples of the book' – Jews and Muslims – have for long periods doubted the legitimacy of making images of real objects. By contrast, Christianity rapidly adapted the artistic traditions of ancient Greece and Rome to its own requirements.

From the 4th century AD, when Christianity became supreme throughout the Roman world, skills and resources were increasingly devoted to religious art. Then, after the collapse of the Roman Empire in the West, the authority and wealth of the Church ensured that this situation remained essentially unchanged for over a thousand years. The Renaissance gave secular works a new status, but only in the 18th century did the long supremacy of religious art come to an end – which is not to say that no worthwhile examples have been produced since then.

Religious art has taken many forms – mosaic, stained glass and sculpture, and painting on manuscripts (miniatures), panels, canvases and walls. It has also fulfilled many functions, providing picture 'texts' for the illiterate, as well as beautifying objects and buildings. In time, the buildings included the homes of laymen. By the late Middle Ages, secular patronage was becoming increasingly important, leading to the creation of objects such as altarpieces in which the donors were portrayed in the company of the Virgin or saints, neatly combining piety with display.

In the past, most artists were told what subject to paint, and were expected to work within a set of widely accepted conventions; on occasion, a church or monastery might be even more demanding, laying down the number of angels to be included or the range of colours and amount of gold to be used. Later, religious and social changes made it possible for an artist to work in a personal style and even develop a personal, perhaps heterodox, vision; the English artist William Blake (page 40) is a prime example. However, it must also be said that the Bible is full of good stories – including sexual adventures – and that not every biblical painting is entirely spiritual in its inspiration.

Religious works are generally saturated in the atmosphere of the period in which they were created; examples are the French classicism of Poussin (page 26) and the Victorian sentimentality of Holman Hunt (page 48). A sense of history is a relatively late development, and many artists have shown biblical characters in costumes and settings like those of their own contemporaries, a practice which served in its time to make the event portrayed seem more vital and relevant.

Much religious art is not directly drawn from the Bible. It includes legends which have since grown up round biblical events, the post-biblical teachings of the churches, and the entire 2000-year-old history of Christianity. All of these have been excluded from this book, since the material based directly upon biblical narratives is already super-abundant. Even great favourites such as the Madonna and Child (that is, a 'double portrait' unconnected with a specific biblical event) have been excluded. The pictures are arranged so that they follow the chronology of the Bible, irrespective of when they were painted.

There are now many editions of the Bible translated into contemporary idiomatic English. For our purposes it seemed more appropriate to present quotations in the majestic 17th century prose of the Authorized Version (King James Bible), itself one of the greatest works of all religious art.

△ **The Creation of the Sun and Moon** 1512
Michelangelo Buonarroti (1475-1564)

Fresco

THE FIRST BOOK of the Bible, Genesis, opens with the declaration that 'In the beginning God created the heaven and the earth. And the earth was without form, and void; and darkness was upon the face of the deep. And the Spirit of God moved upon the face of the waters. And God said, Let there be light; and there was light.' He then separated day from night, and went on to make the plants and creatures before creating a man. Understandably, artistic representations of these tremendous events are relatively rare. But the most titanic figure of the Italian Renaissance, Michelangelo, executed a cycle of paintings in which he attempted to capture something of the cosmic splendour of the Creation: *The Separation of the Light from the Darkness, The Creation of the Sun and Moon, God separating the Waters from the Earth, The Creation of Adam and The Creation of Eve*. Moreover these are only a small part of his work on the Sistine Chapel ceiling, which is often regarded as the greatest human act of creation.

▷ The Garden of Eden c.1515
Hieronymus Bosch (c.1450-1516)

Panel

GOD, HAVING MADE EARTH and heaven, fashioned a man from the dust of the ground, which was still barren. 'And the Lord God planted a garden eastward in Eden; and there He put the man whom He had formed. And out of the ground made the Lord God to grow every tree that is pleasant to the sight and good for food.' The man was placed in the garden and, since 'it is not good that the man should be alone', God made a woman from one of the man's ribs while he slept. Eden is one of many visions of a long-lost Golden Age, found in the myths and religions of many cultures. Bosch, an artist of the Netherlands school, is known for his scenes of grotesque and arcane fantasy; the peaceful Eden shown here is the first panel of a triptych which contrasts innocence with a scene in a licentious 'Garden of Delights' and a lurid picture of the hellish torments which are its reward.

◁ **The Fall of Adam** c.1470
Hugo van der Goes
(c.1440-82)

Panel

'AND THE LORD GOD commanded the man, saying, Of every tree of the garden thou mayest freely eat: but of the tree of the knowledge of good and evil, thou shalt not eat of it; for in the day thou eatest thereof thou shalt surely die.' But the serpent persuaded Eve that she and Adam would not die if they ate the fruit, but would become 'like gods'. Eve ate, and then gave some to her husband to eat. This was the Fall, an event put forward in the Bible to explain the existence of toil and suffering. In Christianity its significance was, if anything, still greater, since this Original Sin was regarded as infecting all future humanity. The Flemish painter van der Goes seems to have been an early example of the neurotic genius, despite the cool loveliness of his work (see also page 42). The serpent is not the traditional snake but a disturbing hybrid; its evident femininity perhaps intended to reinforce the misogynistic implications of the Fall.

▷ The Expulsion of Adam and Eve c.1425
Masaccio (1401-28?)

Fresco

HAVING EATEN THE FRUIT of the
knowledge of good and evil,
Adam and Eve and the serpent
were all punished. The serpent
was condemned to crawl upon
its belly, the woman to bring
forth children in pain, and the
man to labour for his food.
Adam and Eve became mortal,
and were driven from the
Garden of Eden. Evoking the
last extremity of anguish and
shame, the fresco by Masaccio
is one of a group of his
paintings in Florence which
revolutionized western art.
During a career lasting only
seven years, Masaccio
abandoned stylized medieval
forms and created solid human
figures and intensely dramatic
scenes, ushering in the
Renaissance. Then, summoned
to work in Rome, he left
Florence and was never heard
of again. Although Adam and
Eve are described as feeling
ashamed of their nakedness
once they had tasted the
forbidden fruit, Masaccio
broke with medieval
convention by showing
their loins.

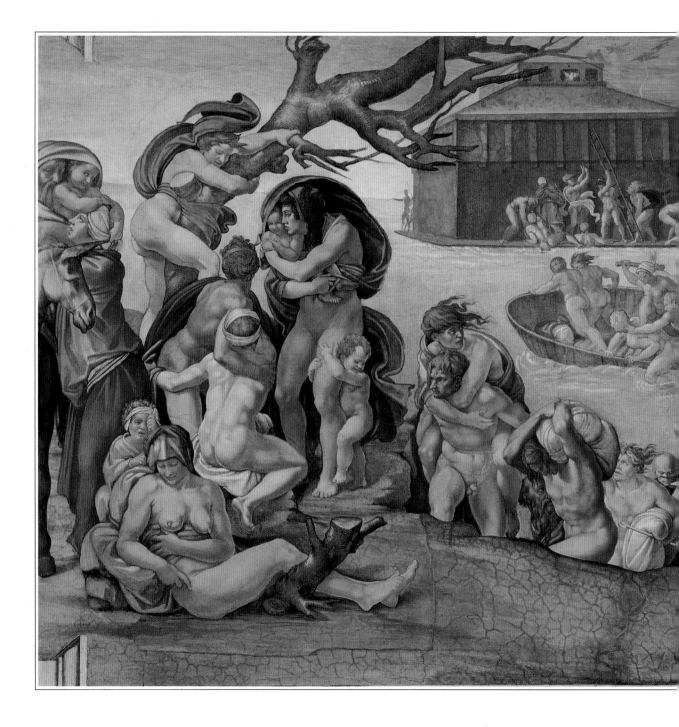

The Deluge 1509
Michelangelo Buonarroti
(1475-1564)

Fresco

◁ *Previous pages 12-13*

GRIEVED AND ANGERED by the wickedness of the human race, God decided to blot out the entire living creation. 'But Noah found favour in the eyes of the Lord', who commanded him to build an ark – a large roofed vessel – and take on board his immediate family and two creatures, a male and a female, of every kind. Noah did as God commanded, and after seven days 'all the fountains of the great deep burst forth, and the windows of the heavens were opened'. Only the inhabitants of the ark survived, eventually issuing forth on Mount Ararat to re-people the earth. *The Deluge* is only one scene among many in Michelangelo's 520-square-metre painting on the ceiling of the Sistine Chapel in Rome, a virtually single-handed enterprise which took almost four years to complete.

▷ The Tower of Babel 1563
Pieter Bruegel the Elder
(c.1520-69)

Panel

AFTER THE DELUGE, the descendants of Noah eventually reached the Land of Shinar, or Babylonia. According to the Old Testament, the hunter Nimrod founded the city of Babylon, of whose name 'Babel' is a variation; and the biblical account of the Tower of Babel undoubtedly draws on memories of the great buildings of ancient Mesopotamia. When the people presumptuously began to build 'a tower whose top may reach unto heaven', God decided to thwart them, by causing them to speak in a variety of tongues. Unable to understand one another, they could no longer work together and spread out over the earth. The Flemish artist Pieter Bruegel shows the tower as a mighty construction, its arcading and cut-away sections perhaps suggested by the ruinous parts of a building at which people still marvelled, the Colosseum in Rome.

◁ **The Angel preventing Abraham from Sacrificing Isaac** 1635
Rembrandt van Rijn (1606-69)

Canvas

ABRAHAM WAS THE FIRST of the Hebrew patriarchs. He made a covenant with God, who promised him that he would become the father of a great nation; but his wife Sarah remained barren for many years. Isaac was the child of Sarah's old age, and God put Abraham to his severest test by ordering him to 'Take your son, your only son Isaac, whom you love, and go to the land of Moriah and offer him as a burnt offering upon one of the mountains'. Abraham showed himself perfectly obedient, and it was only at the last moment that God intervened by sending an angel to countermand the order. In this painting, the great Dutch master Rembrandt heightens the drama: Abraham has pushed back his son's head, baring his throat to the knife, but the Angel of the Lord has gripped the patriarch by the wrist, causing the knife to fall to the ground.

△ **Isaac Blessing Jacob** 1660s
Bartolome Esteban Murillo (1618-82)

Canvas

THIS IS A SCENE of successful deception, practised at the deathbed of Isaac, the son of Abraham. Isaac had twin sons, Esau and Jacob, by his wife Rebecca. As the oldest, Esau was entitled to a double share of the inheritance but, returning hungry and impatient from a hunting trip, he traded his birthright for a dish of lentils – the well-known 'mess of pottage'. When the dying Isaac sent Esau out to slay a deer and bring him a venison stew, Rebecca arranged for her favourite, Jacob, to pretend to be his brother. Murillo's painting shows how the trick was worked: Jacob offered a stew prepared by his mother, and then covered his arm with a goatskin so that his blind father would believe that he was touching the hairy Esau. Thus it was Jacob who received the blessing 'Let people serve thee, and nations bow down to thee' and became the ancestor of the Israelites. Murillo, a Spaniard, was a master of biblical and everyday scenes (genre) in which realism was softened by sentiment.

▷ **The Vision after the Sermon** 1888
Paul Gauguin (1848-1903)

Canvas

GAUGUIN IS BEST KNOWN for the works he painted in Tahiti and the Marquesas, but *The Vision after the Sermon* dates from the important earlier period when he was forming his distinctive style. The biblical event is presented indirectly, as a vision seen by a group of Breton women who have just heard a sermon on the subject of Jacob wrestling with the angel. After fourteen years spent working at Haran for his father-in-law, Laban, Jacob was on his way back to Canaan when he encountered a stranger, usually interpreted as having been an angel. The two wrestled all night, and at daybreak, when the angel failed to overcome Jacob's resistance, he gave him the new name Israel; in the event, the twelve tribes would descend from the twelve sons of Jacob.

◁ **Joseph being sold by his Brothers** 1816
Johann Friedrich Overbeck (1789-1869)

Canvas

JOSEPH WAS THE SON of Jacob and his wife Rachel. Favoured by his father and, if his own dreams were to be believed, destined for greatness, Joseph was envied and disliked by his older half-brothers. When he visited them while they were looking after Jacob's flock, they were tempted to murder him but instead cast him into a pit and sold him to some passing merchants, telling Jacob that he had been slain by wild animals and showing him Joseph's coat, stained with goat's blood, as evidence.

Meanwhile the merchants sold Joseph to the Egyptian Potiphar, the captain of pharaoh's guard. After various vicissitudes Joseph became the most powerful man in Egypt and brought his entire family to live there. Overbeck was one of a group of German painters, the Nazarenes, who in 1810 attempted to revive religious art by forming a brotherhood and working together in Rome; among others, they influenced the British Pre-Raphaelite Brotherhood.

691.

◁ **Moses Rescued from the Nile** c.1580
Veronese (c.1528-88)

Canvas

THANKS TO JOSEPH (page 21), the children of Israel settled in Egypt. But a later pharaoh 'who did not know Joseph' became hostile to this vigorous minority. The Hebrews were used as slave labour on his building programme, and when this failed to break them, Pharaoh ordered that every newborn Hebrew male should be cast into the Nile. One mother managed to conceal her son's existence for three months. When this was no longer possible she made a basket of bulrushes, placed the child in it, and left it on the edge of the Nile. Pharaoh's daughter noticed the basket and, although she realized that the child must be a Hebrew, was moved to adopt him. The painting by Veronese is characteristic of his Venetian delight in colour and courtly magnificence; Pharaoh's daughter is patently a grand 16th century lady, arguably a suitable contemporary equivalent to the Egyptian original.

▷ **Moses defending the daughters of Jethro** c.1525
Rosso Fiorentino (1494-1540)

Canvas

MOSES SLEW AN EGYPTIAN whom he discovered beating a fellow-Hebrew, and fled to Midian. When he saw women being driven from a well by some shepherds, Moses fought off the aggressors and helped the women to draw water. When the women told their father, Jethro, he treated Moses as a guest and eventually married him to one of his daughters, Zipporah. Moses remained in Midian until God spoke to him from a burning bush, ordering him to bring the Israelites out of Egypt. Although the Bible does not describe the confrontation between Moses and the shepherds, Fiorentino turns it into a tremendous fight. The exaggeratedly dynamic composition is characteristic of one strand in late Renaissance painting, deriving from Michelangelo. Rosso emigrated to France, where he worked for the king; he is an important figure in the spread of Renaissance styles from Italy into the rest of Europe.

Moses dividing the Waters of the Red Sea
John Martin (1789-1854)

Canvas

◁ *Previous pages 24-25*

ARMED BY GOD with miraculous powers, Moses was able to stand up to Pharaoh and confound his priests and magicians. A series of plagues, culminating in the deaths of all the first-born children in the land, finally convinced Pharaoh to allow the Hebrews to leave Egypt. But he soon regretted his decision and sent an army in pursuit. When it caught up with the Hebrews, on the shores of the Red Sea, God commanded Moses to raise his hand over the sea: the waters divided, and Moses led his people over dry land to the other side. But when the Egyptians followed, the walls of water fell in on them and every man perished. The English painter John Martin was something of a specialist in apocalyptic subjects, filling his canvases with natural and supernatural cataclysms which dwarf the human participants.

▷ The Adoration of the Golden Calf c.1636
Nicolas Poussin (c.1594-1665)

Canvas

DELIVERED FROM BONDAGE in Egypt under Moses' leadership, the Hebrews spent forty years in the wilderness before they were permitted to enter the Promised Land. A crucial episode involved the handing down of the tablets of the Law, with the Ten Commandments. After forty days on Mount Sinai, Moses came down bearing the stones 'with the writing of God, graven upon the tables', only to find the people worshipping a Golden Calf. In his anger Moses flung down the tablets, smashing them; later, however, he interceded with God, who finally forgave the Hebrews. Poussin shows the backsliders as graceful dancers and revellers, with Aaron in white presiding over the festivities; on the left, Moses, coming down from the mountains, shatters the tablets. Despite the great beauty of its design, it is hard not to view this as anything but a picture of harmless arcadian merrymaking.

◁ **Samson and Delilah** c.1610
Peter Paul Rubens (1577-1640)

Panel

SAMSON'S NAME has become a
byword for immense strength.
He was the superhero and
judge who championed the
Israelites against the
Philistines. His exploits
included the slaughter of a
thousand men when he was
armed with nothing but the
jawbone of an ass. Samson's
love affair with a Philistine
woman, Delilah, caused his
downfall. Bribed to discover
the secret of his strength, she
cross-questioned him until,
'vexed unto death', he told her
the truth: that the secret lay in
his hair, which he must never
cut. Delilah lulled Samson to
sleep, sheared off his locks,
and delivered him to his
enemies, who blinded him and
set him to work a treadmill.
This tale of love and betrayal
has appealed to artists more
than Samson's eventual
redemption; Rembrandt
painted the hero's blinding,
while the exuberant Flemish
master Rubens has captured a
before-and-after moment
which brilliantly combines the
sensual and the sinister.

The Young David c.1451 Andrea del Castagno (c.1418-57)

Paint on leather

◁ *Previous page 29*

DAVID, THE YOUNGER SON of a farmer, seemed an unlikely candidate for greatness. But 'God was with him', and he was sought out and anointed as the king-to-be by the prophet Samuel. Ignorant of the events to come, the actual king, Saul, summoned the youth to his court, finding relief from his depressions in listening to David playing on the harp. Then, when the Philistines attacked Israel, the mighty Goliath challenged any Israelite to meet him in single combat. Only David dared to do so, slaying Goliath with a single shot from his sling. Andrea del Castagno, an Italian Renaissance artist, gave his painting its unusual shape because its leather surface was intended to cover a shield. He shows David in action, one arm raised to steady and guide the sling he is about to use; the outcome is anticipated by the placing of Goliath's severed head between the young hero's feet.

▷ **Bathsheba holding King David's Letter** 1654 Rembrandt van Rijn (1606-69)

Canvas

AFTER THE DEATH OF SAUL, Israel was racked by a civil war from which David emerged victorious over Saul's heirs. David's forty-year reign as king of Israel was a considerable political success, although it was marred by murderous family feuds. The king's headstrong and ruthless streak appeared when he saw the lovely Bathsheba, wife of Uriah the Hittite, bathing, and at once sent a message to her. She lay with him and became pregnant; and when the king's scheme to pass the responsibility on to her absent husband failed, he sent Uriah into the front line of a battle and made sure that he was deserted by his comrades and slain. In one of his finest works, Rembrandt has given dignity to the sordid story, picturing Bathsheba at the moment when she has received David's letter and is pondering, and perhaps deciding, the nature of her destiny.

◁ **The Queen of Sheba visits Solomon** 1450s
Piero della Francesca
(c.1418-92)

Fresco

SOLOMON WAS THE SON of King David and Bathsheba. When he became king, Solomon built the Temple in Jerusalem and became renowned for his wisdom and power. The queen of Sheba, or Saba, a land on the east coast of the Red Sea, decided to see this prodigy for herself. She travelled in great style, her camels carrying presents of spices, gold and precious stones for Solomon. When they met, he answered all the 'hard questions' she had prepared, and the queen admitted that his reputation was fully justified. Although damaged, Piero's fresco is a wonderfully sober, stately Renaissance version of the meeting. The scene on the left is based on the later christian legend that the Queen knelt in adoration after a revelation that the wood of the local bridge would be used in Jesus' crucifixion.

◁ **Elijah and the Widow's Son**
1864
Ford Madox Brown (1821-93)

Canvas

PROPHET AND MIRACLE-WORKER, Elijah fearlessly opposed the idolatries of Ahab, the King of Israel, and his Sidonian queen, Jezebel. During a terrible drought brought down upon Israel by Ahab's sinfulness, Elijah was at first fed by ravens beside the brook Cherith; then he was ordered by God to dwell with a widow who lived at Zarepath. There, they had enough to live on since, miraculously, the contents of the widow's jar of meal and cruse of oil were never exhausted. But soon the widow's son fell ill and died. When she reproached Elijah, he 'stretched himself upon the child three times' and appealed to the Lord, 'and the soul of the child came into him again, and he revived'. The English painter Ford Madox Brown chooses to represent the moment immediately after the miracle, when Elijah brought the child down from the upper chamber to his rejoicing mother.

▷ **The Toilet of Esther** 1842
Theodore Chassériau
(1819-56)

Canvas

WHEN THE PERSIAN KING
Ahasuerus (Xerxes) put away
his wife for disobedience, he
held a kind of beauty
competition and eventually
chose Esther as his new
consort, not knowing that she
was Jewish. The Book of
Esther describes how Esther's
adopted father, Mordecai,
offended the king's chief
adviser, Haman, who schemed
to do away with him and wipe
out all the Jews in the empire.
Thanks to Esther's courage,
and the king's love for her, the
tables were turned and Haman
was hanged from the gallows
he had prepared for Mordecai.
The episode came to symbolize
the dangers that threatened
the Jewish people throughout
their history, and their ability
to surmount them. The
French painter Chassériau was
a pupil and follower of Ingres.
Here, the subject is little more
than an excuse for sensual
orientalism of a kind that was
fashionable at the time.

◁ **Tobias and the Angel**
c.1469
Antonio Pollaiuolo
(c.1432-98)

Panel

AS CIRCUMSTANTIAL and exciting as a modern short story, the Book of Tobit begins with a first-person account of the unjust persecution and blinding of Tobit, a Jew living in ancient Nineveh. But when Tobit sends his son Tobias to collect an old debt, the young man encounters the archangel Raphael, disguised as a fellow-countryman, and the two travel together. When Tobias catches a large fish, Raphael persuades him to save its gall, heart and liver. At the house of a kinsman, Tobias falls in love with his cousin Sara, despite the fact that she is haunted by a demon that has killed each of her seven previous bridegrooms. With the help of the fish heart and liver, Tobias drives off the demon. Then, back at home, he anoints his father's eyes with the gall, and his sight is restored. Pollaiuolo, a leading Italian Renaissance artist, treats the subject in a characteristically virile fashion.

Judith and Holofernes c.1620
Artemisia Gentileschi (1593-1652)

Canvas

◁ *Previous page 37*

JUDITH IS SAID to have been a beautiful Jewish widow who lived in the city of Bethulia. When it was besieged by the forces of the Babylonian king Nebuchadnezzar, she managed to secure an interview with the enemy commander, Holofernes, pretending she had secrets to reveal. She skilfully led him on while plying him with drink, until Holofernes fell into a drunken slumber. Then she cut off his head and escaped with it to show her people; they were filled with new courage and drove off the invaders. The subject was a popular one with painters, but few emphasized the savagery of the killing with such relish as Artemisia Gentileschi, one of the very few women before the 18th century who were able to overcome their social handicaps and make a substantial contribution to art. Her treatment of the subject may have been influenced by her turbulent career in a male-dominated world.

▷ Susanna and the Elders c.1560
Tintoretto (1518-94)

Canvas

SUSANNA WAS A BEAUTIFUL married woman who belonged to the Jewish community living in Babylonia. Two elders spied on her while she was bathing. Then they confronted her, demanding that she lie with them, threatening to bear false witness against her if she refused. Susanna told them to do their worst, but when they charged her with committing adultery she was sentenced to death. The young prophet Daniel saved her by questioning the elders separately and showing up the contradictions between their accounts. The tale comes from the Apocrypha, the collection of stories whose biblical credentials have been disputed. Painters have been attracted to Susanna's story because of its dramatic and erotic interest. The Venetian Tintoretto makes Susanna a figure of Renaissance opulence, dwelling on her beauty aids and turning the elders into figures of fun.

△ **Nebuchadnezzar** 1795
William Blake (1757-1827)

Print

THE BABYLONIAN KING Nebuchadnezzar plays an ambiguous role in the Book of Daniel. He is the conqueror of Jerusalem and the destroyer of the Temple; but he also employs Daniel and his friends, and has an intermittent sense of God's power, shown when Shadrach, Mesach and Abednego pass safely through the fiery furnace. Later, having ignored one of Daniel's prophecies, he lost his reason. 'He was driven from men, and did eat grass as oxen, and his body was wet with the dew of heaven, till his hairs were grown like eagles' feathers, and his nails like birds' claws.' He is shown at his most degraded in this print by William Blake, an English artist and poet whose intense, visionary style reflected his own otherworldly experiences. After seven years Nebuchadnezzar recovered, repented, and received back his kingdom.

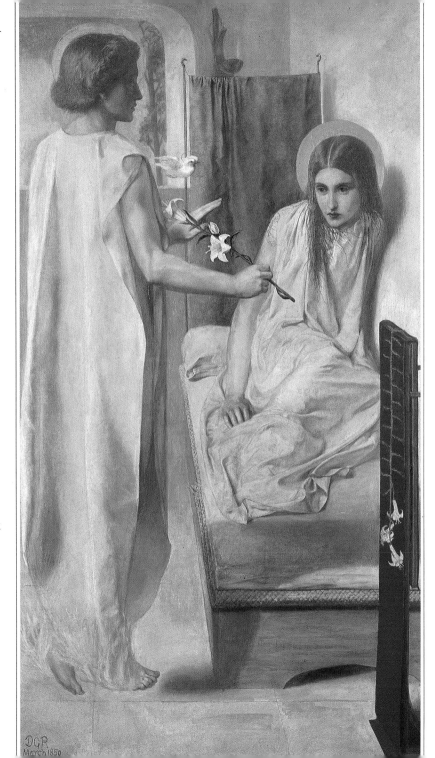

▷ **Ecce Ancilla Domini** 1850
Dante Gabriel Rossetti
(1828-82)

Canvas

FOR CENTURIES, every
Christian artist of note painted
this scene, commonly known
as the Annunciation; Rossetti's
title means 'Behold the
handmaiden of the Lord', but
the subject is the traditional
one. The angel Gabriel has
sought out Mary, a virgin
betrothed to the carpenter
Joseph, saying 'Hail, thou that
art highly favoured, the Lord
is with thee: blessed art thou
among women.' He tells her
that she will conceive a son
whom she must call Jesus, and
that 'of his kingdom there
shall be no end'. Unmarried,
Mary is at first disturbed by
the news, and traditionally
Annunciation scenes show her
tending to shrink away from
Gabriel. With Millais and Hunt
(page 49), Rossetti founded
the Pre-Raphaelite
Brotherhood in 1848, aiming
to bring a new freshness,
seriousness and sincerity to
English art. And in fact the
informality of Mary's pose on
the bed seemed audacious and
even blasphemous to mid-19th
century taste.

▷ The Adoration of the Shepherds c.1475
Hugo van der Goes (c.1440-82)

Panel

THE GOSPELS give two somewhat different accounts of the Nativity. Luke's story is the more circumstantial, relating how Joseph and Mary left Nazareth for Bethlehem in order to register for the census decreed by Caesar Augustus. While they were there, Mary gave birth in a stable, laying the new-born child in a manger. An angel came to some shepherds in the neighbourhood who were keeping watch over their flocks, telling them of the birth of the Messiah and directing them to the manger. Hugo van der Goes, the greatest Flemish artist of his day, pictures the ensuing scene. With the animals behind her as interested spectators, Mary gazes down at her vulnerable but radiant child. Angels surround him, but the shepherds are completely human, rough enough fellows who are struck with wonder at what they see. The scene was painted on the central panel of an altarpiece sent to Florence, where van der Goes' skilful use of oils did much to popularize the medium and influence the course of the Italian Renaissance.

◁ The Adoration of the Magi
1504
Albrecht Durer (1471-1528)

Panel

ST MATTHEW'S VERSION of the Nativity emphasizes the role of the Magi, wise men who arrived in Jerusalem from the East. They inquired where they could find the child destined to be the king of the Jews. Recalling prophecies, King Herod directed them to Bethlehem, asking them to report back – with the secret intention of eliminating a threat to his authority. The Magi followed the star to Bethlehem. Over the centuries the Gospel story was elaborated: in the Catholic West, the number of the Magi was fixed at three, and they were named as Caspar, Melchior and Balthazar (traditionally portrayed as black). Later still the Magi were transformed into kings. Artists took the opportunity to contrast the humble surroundings of the Holy Family with the rich apparel of the Magi/Kings; this example, by the great German painter and engraver Durer, is typical of the Renaissance approach to the subject.

The Flight into Egypt c.1450
Fra Angelico (c.1400/55?)

Panel

▷ *Overleaf page 46*

AFTER WORSHIPPING the baby Jesus, the Magi returned home without reporting to Herod. But Joseph was warned in a dream to take his family to safety in Egypt. While they were gone, Herod ordered the murder of all the small children in Bethlehem (the Massacre of the Innocents). After Herod's death, another angel told Joseph to return, and the family settled at Nazareth in Galilee, where Jesus grew up. Paintings of the flight into Egypt range from imaginary pursuit scenes to family portraits in landscape settings. Fra Angelico ('the Angelic Brother') was the nickname of a Dominican friar, Fra Giovanni da Fiesole. His work combines a singularly sweet piety with the sophisticated perspective and other technical discoveries of the early Renaissance. He travelled widely, but his most celebrated works were executed on the cell walls of the Dominican priory of San Marco in Florence.

SVRGE ACCIPE PVERVM 7 MATREM. EP 7 FVGE INEGIPTVM .MACEI. II. C.

◁ **The Presentation in the Temple** c.1470
Hans Memling (c.1433-94)

Panel

LIKE EVERY CHILD of orthodox Jews, Jesus was circumcised when he was eight days old. Shortly afterwards he was brought to Jerusalem and, as the first-born son of Joseph and Mary, presented (given) to the Lord in the Temple. Simeon, a pious old man was also there. It had been revealed to him that before he died he would see the Messiah, and when Joseph and Mary appeared with Jesus, he took the child in his arms and praised God for fulfilling the prophecy. On this occasion Anna, a prophetess, also recognized Jesus as the Messiah. Memling (or Memlinc) was born in Germany, but belonged to the Flemish school of painting, spending his working life at Bruges; he is said to have been a pupil of Rogier van der Weyden (page 71). His grave, rather unimpassioned version of the scene is typical of his style.

The Finding of the Saviour in the Temple 1860
William Holman Hunt (1827-1910)

Canvas

◁ *Previous pages 48-49*

WHEN JESUS WAS TWELVE years old, his parents made their annual Passover visit to Jerusalem. On the way back to Nazareth they realized that he was not among their company. Returning to Jerusalem, they found the boy with the learned men in the Temple, listening to them and questioning them with an understanding that amazed all who heard him. When his mother reproached him, Jesus answered 'How is it that ye sought me? Wist ye not that I must be about my Father's business?' Holman Hunt, one of the original founders of the Pre-Raphaelite Brotherhood (with Millais and Rossetti, page 41), visited Egypt and Palestine several times in order to make the settings of his works as authentic as possible. Unlike most of his contemporaries, he shows Jesus as a child of the Levant, but the sentimental treatment of the scene is very much of its period.

▷ The Baptism of Christ
c.1445
Piero della Francesca
(c.1418-92)

Panel

ONE OF THE MOST intriguing personalities in the Gospels, John the Baptist was the son of the Virgin Mary's cousin Elizabeth. John wandered through the valley of the River Jordan, urging the people to repent, and to demonstrate their repentance by being baptized. When the people began to wonder whether he was the expected Messiah, he made it clear that he was the forerunner of a greater being. Jesus was baptized by John, an event imagined by Piero in the altarpiece panel painted for the priory of St John the Baptist in his native Sansepolcro, Umbria. Three angels look on as John pours water over Jesus, while a dove with outspread wings hovers above. Despite the presence of another candidate for baptism who is in the middle of undressing, the scene has a majestic stillness that is Piero's hallmark. No contemporary evidence exists to date it, but it is generally thought to have been one of his early works.

◁ **Salome** 1876
Gustav Moreau (1826-98)

Canvas

ONE OF THE MOST sensational of biblical stories is that of Salome's dance and the death of St John the Baptist; many artists have been attracted to it. In pursuit of his mission (see page 50), John denounced the marriage of Herodias to Herod Antipas, tetrarch of Galilee, on the grounds that she had already been the wife of his half-brother. Herod arrested John, but the prophet was not harmed until Herodias' daughter, Salome, danced before him at his birthday banquet. Herod was so delighted that he promised to grant her anything she asked for; and she demanded the Baptist's head on a platter. The French painter Gustave Moreau presents a visionary rather than a literal version of the event, which he invests with a sinister glamour; his work strongly influenced the 'decadents' of the late 19th century, many of whom (including Oscar Wilde and Aubrey Beardsley) elaborated perverse interpretations of the Salome story.

▷ **The Marriage Feast at Cana**
Juan de Flandes (died c.1519)

Panel

JESUS' FIRST MIRACLE was performed at Cana, a village in Galilee not far from Nazareth. When the wine ran out at a marriage feast, Jesus ordered the servants to fill six large jars with water, draw off the contents, which had turned to wine, and sent it to the steward in charge of the festivities. When the steward tasted it, he praised what he imagined to be the bridegroom's largesse: 'Every man at the beginning doth set forth good wine; and when men have well drunk, then that which is worse: but thou hast kept the good wine until now.' The best-known painting of the subject is by Veronese (page 22), who interprets it as a lavish banquet for Venetian grandees. But the grave loveliness of Juan de Flandes' version seems more in keeping with the New Testament spirit. Juan may have come from the Netherlands, but the little that is known of him concerns his work in Spain from 1496.

◁ **Christ in the House of Martha and Mary**
Probably 1650s
Jan Vermeer (1632-75)

Canvas

AT BETHANY, a village outside Jerusalem, Jesus made friends with the sisters Mary and Martha and their brother Lazarus. When the sisters entertained Jesus in their home, Mary sat at his feet and listened to his words, while Martha busied herself preparing and serving food. When Martha complained about her sister's idleness, Jesus rebuked her gently and indicated that Mary had chosen the better part. Two subsequent episodes centred on this family: Jesus' raising of Lazarus from the dead; and Mary's anointing of Jesus' feet, which she then dried with her hair. Jan Vermeer of Delft seems to have lived and died in quiet obscurity, and only in the 19th century did his exquisite poetic interiors begin to be appreciated. *Christ in the House of Martha and Mary* is generally held to be an early example of his work.

▷ **The Return of the Prodigal Son** c.1668
Rembrandt van Rijn (1606-69)

Canvas

ON MANY OCCASIONS Jesus instructed his hearers through parables – homely tales with a moral that could be applied to spiritual matters. One of the most celebrated parables describes how a younger son insists upon cashing in his inheritance while his father is still alive. He squanders it in a distant land and falls into misery. Finally he realizes that he would be better off as a servant in his father's house than as a starveling among strangers and, abjectly penitent, makes his way home. But when he approaches, his father rejoices, orders the preparation of a feast, and soothes the resentment felt by his dutiful elder son. The story was intended to show that God would never shut the door against those who repented, however sinful they might have been. Rembrandt pictures the homecoming as a moment of intense tenderness between the aged father and the prodigal in the worn-out remains of his finery.

▷ **The Woman taken in Adultery** c.1621
Il Guercino (1591-1666)

Canvas

In Jerusalem, the scribes and Pharisees hostile to Jesus brought before him a woman who had been caught in adultery, 'in the very act'. Reminding Jesus that Moses laid down stoning as the appropriate punishment for adultery, they asked for his opinion, probably hoping that he would be torn between condoning a punishment that had fallen into disuse, and contradicting the most revered of Hebrew religious leaders. Instead, Jesus declared, 'He that is without sin among you, let him first cast a stone at her.' Smitten by their consciences, his opponents slunk away, and Jesus told the woman herself to go away and sin no more. 'Il Guercino' ('squint-eye') was the nickname of the Bolognese painter Giovanni Francisco Barbieri.

◁ **Christ driving the Traders from The Temple** c.1600
El Greco (1541-1614)

Canvas

SOON AFTER ENTERING Jerusalem mounted on a donkey, Jesus went to the Temple. He overturned the tables of the money changers and pigeon-vendors, whom he drove away, saying 'It is written, My house shall be called a house of prayer; but ye have made it a den of thieves.' A scene of such violent action appealed to artists of the post-Renaissance period, who had a taste for unusual and dynamic effects. Arguably the greatest painter of the period was El Greco ('the Greek'), born Domenikos Theotocopoulos in Crete, who spent most of his working life in Spain. His elongated figures, strong colours and emphatic silvery highlighting always create a strange, otherworldly atmosphere, here combined with a masterful depiction of vehemence and movement.

▷ **The Last Supper** (detail) 1447
Andrea del Castagno (c.1418-57)

Fresco

AT PASSOVER, on the day before his arrest and crucifixion, Jesus had a final meal with his disciples at which he passed round wine and broke bread which he invited them to share, saying 'This is my body.' Then he told them that the man who would betray him was present in the room, and hinted at the nature of his fate. A painting of the Last Supper was commonly hung in the refectory of a religious community, and as a result many ambitious versions of the subject exist; the most famous of all (unfortunately only a noble ruin) is by Leonardo da Vinci. In this detail of Castagno's masterpiece, painted for a convent in Florence, Judas is shown in traditional fashion, without a halo and on the opposite side of the table from Jesus and the other disciples; Castagno has even made the betrayer's features unmistakeably diabolic. John has fallen fast asleep. Jesus' hand is raised over the bread and wine – of which Judas has already taken a piece, which consequently remains unblessed.

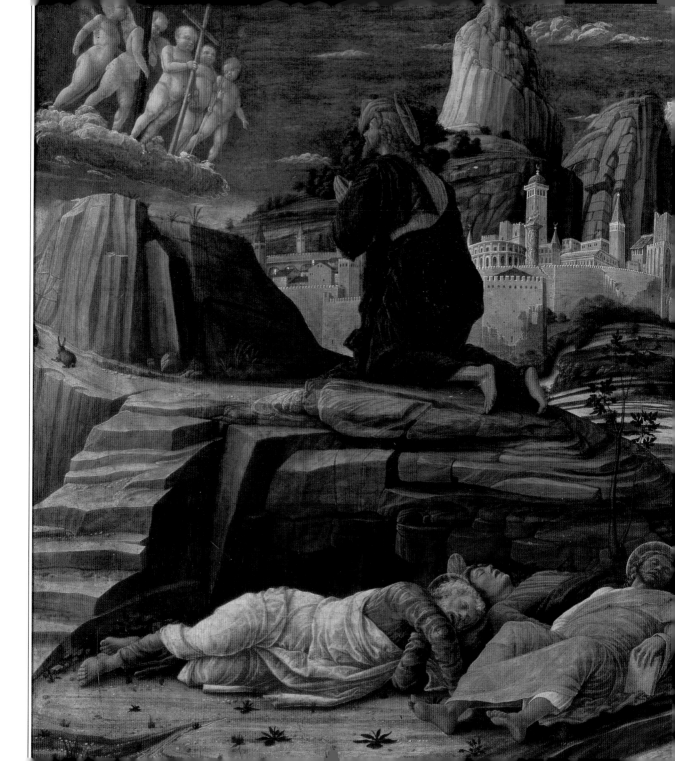

◁ **The Agony in the Garden**
c.1455
Andrea Mantegna
(c.1431-1506)

Panel

JESUS SPENT THE NIGHT before
his arrest and execution in the
garden of Gethsemane, just
outside Jerusalem. Peter,
James and John came with
him to watch and pray, but in
spite of their good intentions
they fell asleep. Preparing for
the ordeal to come, Jesus
prayed, even momentarily
hoping that it might be
avoided: 'Abba, Father, all
things are possible unto thee:
take away this cup from me:
nevertheless not what I will,
but what thou wilt.' In
Mantegna's masterpiece the
angels display a cross to Jesus;
Roman soldiers, led by Judas,
are already on their way to
make the arrest. Mantegna was
one of the outstanding Italian
Renaissance artists of his time,
creating scenes of a hardness
and clarity reminiscent of
sculpture. In the background
stands Jerusalem, splendidly
imagined as an ideal
Renaissance or classical city.

▷ **St Peter's Denial** 1650
Georges de La Tour
(1593-1652)

Canvas

AFTER THE SOLDIERS had
arrested Jesus, Peter followed
them at a distance. They took
their prisoner into the house
of the high priest, while Peter
joined a group in the
courtyard. When a serving
maid suggested that he had
been with Jesus, Peter denied
all knowledge of his master.
The same thing happened a
second, and then a third time.
As Peter uttered his third
denial, a cock crowed. Then
the disciple remembered that
at the Last Supper, Jesus had
said 'I tell thee, Peter, the cock
shall not crow this day, before
that thou shalt thrice deny that
thou knowest me.' Yet despite
his human failings, Peter was
the disciple Jesus most relied
on, and destined to be the
founder of his church. The
entire career of the painter
Georges de La Tour was spent
in Lorraine; his emphatic
contrasts of light and shadow
derive from Caravaggio (page
74), but his monumental style
is distinctively his own.

◁ **What Is Truth?** 1890
Nikolai Nikolaievich Ge
(1831-94)

Canvas

AFTER A HEARING before the high priest, Caiaphas, Jesus was taken to the Roman governor of Judea, Pontius Pilate. The accounts in the Gospels generally show Pilate in a fairly sympathetic light, as an official curious but puzzled, asking the accused man 'Art thou the King of the Jews?' and receiving only the enigmatic reply, 'Thou sayest it.' Finally Pilate was not prepared to risk a riot over a local matter and publicly washed his hands to show that the decision to crucify Jesus was not his. (Modern authorities, however, are sceptical, pointing out that crucifixion was a specifically Roman form of punishment.) In this unusual painting by a 19th century Russian artist, Pilate is shown in the light and Jesus in shadow. Although light is traditionally associated with religious truth, Ge's scheme is thought-provoking, suggesting the contrast between the worldy assurance of one figure and the mysterious spiritual depths of the other.

Christ crowned with Thorns c.1480
Hieronymus Bosch (c.1450-1516)

Panel

◁ *Previous page 67*

CONDEMNED by a reluctant Pontius Pilate to be flogged and crucified, Jesus was put in the charge of a squad of soldiers who took him into a courtyard and made him the butt of their sadistic sense of fun. They wrapped him in a cloak of imperial purple, wove a crown of thorns for his head, hailed him as the king of the Jews and spat on him and beat him about the head. Bosch makes the sadists civilians who might well be Dutch peasants, although they are shown as droolingly grotesque in their malevolence; the way in which they paw their victim is particularly disgusting. Jesus himself appears detached from the proceedings, apparently indifferent to the threatened crowning with thorns, although the 'crown' is so vicious that one of his tormentors holds it in an an armoured fist.

▷ The Crucifixion (detail) c.1512-16
Matthias Grunewald (c.1475-1528)

Panel

JESUS WAS TAKEN to Calvary, or Golgotha, 'the place of the skull', to be crucified between two robbers. The Gospels suggest that he took about six hours to die. From noon, a great darkness is said to have covered the entire land. At about three o'clock Jesus cried out 'My God, my God, why hast thou forsaken me?' Shortly afterwards he uttered a loud cry and died. A soldier checked that he was not still alive by thrusting a spear into his side. Although the Crucifixion has been a central preoccupation of Christian artists, few have charged the scene with such physical horror as Grunewald. Like his fellow-German contemporary Durer (page 45), Grunewald absorbed Renaissance techniques; but he employed them in the emotionally intense Gothic spirit of the North, showing a Christ whose body is tortured, broken and blood-spattered.

◁ **The Deposition** c.1435
Rogier van der Weyden (c.1399-1464)

Panel

THANKS TO THE WEALTHY Joseph of Aramathea, who intervened with Pontius Pilate, Jesus' body was taken down from the cross and decently buried before the Sabbath began. The first physical contacts between the dead Christ and his followers have long been felt to have a special emotional significance, and consequently they have frequently been treated in art – so much so that they have been sub-divided into different but related episodes: the Deposition or Descent from the Cross; the Lamentation over the body as it is laid upon the ground; and the Pietà, showing Mary cradling the dead Christ in her lap. *The Deposition* by the Flemish artist Rogier van der Weyden is a truly extraordinary work, its rich colours and crowded figures creating an almost dance-like rhythm which give it an intense, tragic energy.

◁ **The Resurrection** c.1512-16
Matthias Grunewald
(c.1475-1528)

Panel

WHEN THE SABBATH had
ended, Mary Magdalene and
other women followers of
Jesus went back to the tomb in
which his body had been laid.
They found that the stone
blocking the entrance had
been moved and there was no
sign of the body. In the
account given by the Gospel
According to St Luke, the
women were trying to
understand what had
happened when they became
aware of two men standing by
them 'in shining garments'.
'Why seek ye the living among
the dead?' they asked. 'He is
not here, but is risen.' The
women hurried to tell the
disciples, who were sceptical
until they had verified the facts
for themselves. To judge by
their works, artists have found
it much harder to represent
ecstasies of joy than the depths
of suffering. Appropriately, the
painter of one of the most
terrible Crucifixions also
succeeded triumphantly in
fashioning an image of the
Risen Christ in golden glory.

▷ **Noli Me Tangere** c.1522
Correggio (1489-1534)

Panel

THE GOSPEL ACCORDING to St
John names Mary Magdalene
as the first person to see Jesus
alive after the crucifixion. She
was weeping at his tomb when
he revealed himself, and she at
first mistook him for the
gardener. He commanded her
not to touch him (*Noli Me
Tangere* in the Latin translation
of the Bible), but to hurry away
and warn the disciples of his
imminent ascent to the Father.
Mary had become a follower of
Jesus after he had driven seven
evil spirits out of her, and she
was one of the women present
at the foot of the cross during
his last moments. There is no
biblical basis for the common
identification of Mary as a
penitent prostitute, although
many painters have taken
advantage of it to introduce a
touch of sex and sin into their
works. Correggio (Antonio
Allegri) was nicknamed after
his birthplace in the Emilia
(northern Italy). *Noli Me
Tangere* is notable not only for
the solid, living quality of the
figures, but also for its
beautiful, lushly wooded
background.

▷ **The Supper at Emmaus** c.1600
Michelangelo Merisi da Caravaggio (1573-1610)

Canvas

SOME TIME AFTER the crucifixion, two of Jesus' followers met a stranger who went with them on their journey to Emmaus. Although he interpreted the Scriptures with authority, they did not guess his identity until they had reached the village and settled down for a meal at the inn. When the stranger broke bread for them, their eyes were suddenly opened and they recognized him as Jesus, risen from the dead; whereupon he vanished. Caravaggio was a dubious character who spent the last years of his short life on the run after stabbing a man in Rome. Yet he was a religious artist of stature and created a new, dramatic style of painting based on chiaroscuro (contrasts of light and shadow). The supper at Emmaus ideally suited his talents, and the virtuoso painting of the arms flung out towards the spectator has always been greatly admired.

◁ **The Ascension** 1577
Tintoretto (1518-94)

Canvas

AFTER HIS RESURRECTION, Jesus appeared three times to his disciples: twice in the room where they met, and once while they were fishing in the Sea of Tiberias (the occasion of the miraculous draught of fishes). Finally 'he led them out as far as to Bethany, and he lifted up his hands, and blessed them. And it came to pass, while he blessed them, he was parted from them, and carried up into heaven.' The disciples then returned to Jerusalem with the joyful news. Tintoretto's *Ascension* belongs to an extraordinary cycle of paintings that he executed for the Scuola di San Rocco in his native Venice. The flamboyance and energy, typical of his style, are particularly appropriate here. Christ ascends, escorted by angels; curiously, Tintoretto has made the upper part of the picture more substantial than the earthly scene below, perhaps to imply that the spiritual realm is the more durable.

▷ **The Stoning of St Stephen**
c.1602
Adam Elsheimer (1578-1610)

Copper

ST STEPHEN was the first Christian martyr. His teaching and the miracles he performed, upset the religious authorities, and a false charge of blasphemy was levelled against him. Taken up in front of the council, he antagonized its members by telling them that they and their like had always rejected the prophets, just as they now rejected Jesus. 'Then they cried out with a loud voice, and stopped their ears, and ran upon him with one accord, and cast him out of the city, and stoned him.' Stephen 'kneeled down, and cried with a loud voice, Lord, lay not this sin to their charge. And when he had said this, he fell asleep.' Adam Elsheimer was a German, although most of his working life was spent in Italy; he specialized in small paintings done on copper plates. The rich fabrics, warm landscape background and Roman ruins, though interesting, rather undermine the savagery of the scene.

◁ **The Conversion of St Paul**
1542-45
Michelangelo Buonarroti
(1475-1564)

Fresco

SAUL OF TARSUS was a fanatical persecutor of the early Christians who had witnessed and approved of the martyrdom of Stephen (page 77). He was on the road to Damascus when 'suddenly there shined round about him a light from heaven; and he fell to the earth, and heard a voice saying unto him, Saul, Saul, why persecutest thou me?' His companions brought Saul to Tarsus, where he was blind for three days, until Ananias was instructed by Jesus to cure him. He was baptized and became the Apostle Paul, the greatest of Christian missionaries. Michelangelo's fresco is a work of his old age, commissioned by the Apostle's namesake, Pope Paul II, for the Pauline Chapel in the Vatican. It is in Michelangelo's late style, darker, more troubled and less concerned with physically splendid beings than his Sistine Chapel paintings (page 14). Strangely, he makes Saul an old man, perhaps in compliment to the pope.

ACKNOWLEDGEMENTS

The publisher would like to thank the following for their kind permission to reproduce the paintings in this book:

Bridgeman Art Library, London/Vatican Library, Rome: 8; /**Prado, Madrid**: 9; /**Kunsthistorisches Museum, Vienna**: 10; /**Brancacci Chapel, Santa Maria del Carmine, Florence**: 11; /**Vatican Museums & Galleries, Rome**: 12-13; /**Kunsthistorisches Museum, Vienna**: 14-15; /**Hermitage, St Petersburg**: 16, 17; /**National Gallery of Scotland, Edinburgh**: 18-19; /**Staatliche Museen, Berlin**: 20-21; /**Prado, Madrid**: 22; /**Galleria degli Uffizi, Florence**: 23; /**Victoria & Albert Museum, London**: 24-25; /**National Gallery, London**: 26-27, 28; /**National Gallery of Art, Washington D.C.**: 29; /**Louvre, Paris/Giraudon**: 31; /**Chiesa di S. Francesco, Arezzo**: 32-33; /**Victoria & Albert Museum, London**: 34; /**Louvre, Paris**: 35; /**Galleria Sabaudia, Turin**: 36; /**Galleria degli Uffizi, Florence**: 37; /**Kunsthistorisches Museum, Vienna**: 39; /**Tate Gallery, London**: 40, 41; /**Galleria degli Uffizi, Florence**: 42, 44-45; /**Birmingham City Museums & Art Gallery**: 48-49; /**National Gallery, London**: 51; /**Private Collection**: 52; /**Christie's, London**: 53; /**National Gallery of Scotland, Edinburgh**: 54; /**Hermitage, St Petersburg**: 55; /**Dulwich Picture Gallery, London**: 56-57; /**National Gallery, London**: 58-59; /**San Apollonia, Florence**: 60-61; /**National Gallery, London**: 62-63; /**Musee des Beaux-Arts, Nantes/Giraudon**: 64-65; /**Tretyakov Gallery, Moscow**: 66; /**National Gallery, London**: 67; /**Unterlinden Museum, Colmar, France**: 69; /**Prado, Madrid**: 70; /**Unterlinden Museum, Colmar, France/Giraudon**: 72; /**Prado, Madrid**: 73; /**National Gallery, London**: 74-75; /**Scuola Grande di San Rocco, Venice**: 76; /**National Gallery of Scotland, Edinburgh**: 77; /**Cappella Paolina, Vatican, Rome**: 78